Preservations of a Dying Adolescence

Ella Cofield

Preservations of a Dying Adolescence
Copyright © 2025 by Ella Cofield.

All rights reserved. No part of this publication may be reproduced, distributed, or transmitted in any form or by any means, including photocopying, recording, or other electronic or mechanical methods, without the written consent of the publisher. The only exceptions are for brief quotations included in critical reviews and other noncommercial uses permitted by copyright law.

MILTON & HUGO L.L.C.
4407 Park Ave., Suite 5
Union City, NJ 07087, USA

Website: *www.miltonandhugo.com*
Hotline: *1- 888-778-0033*
Email: *info@miltonandhugo.com*

Ordering Information:
Quantity sales. Special discounts are granted to corporations, associations, and other organizations. For more information on these discounts, please reach out to the publisher using the contact information provided above.

Library of Congress Control Number:	2025906643
ISBN-13: 979-8-89285-404-7	[Paperback Edition]
979-8-89285-405-4	[Hardback Edition]
979-8-89285-403-0	[Digital Edition]

Rev. date: 04/01/2025

Genesis

In a dream I was told
that we're molds
of the same cosmic dust.
That some God
wrote the book of everything
and on these grounds
she dropped down
all the loose leaves.

Everything Everywhere

A choir of cicadas
open the midnight scene.
I stand
with sand
between my toes,
the clawing waves
pulling back the grains,
to whisk
in the shallow waters.
The seagulls sore above
and follow nothing together.
Always following nothing
Together.
With the new moon
resting beside them.

All is born again

I am spellbound by the night
by the silence
and how it's shattered so easily.
The crickets chime in
the cicadas intermission,
even the wind
has something to say.
Telling me that this right here
is an envelope
sent from God-
unseal the lips
and watch the world unfold.

Nirvana

Let our shoulders touch
on the choir stand.
And open our mouths
to let out
one voice.
Let us bury the self
within the union.
To hold your hand in mine
until we don't know
which is which.
Let us sway in rhythm
while we sing a gentle song
and put havoc
down to rest.

cloud watching

when I was a kid,
my hair was always matted to the grass
watching a theater in the sky
the michelin men
dancing polar bears
white whales
women in skirts
and men with canes
taking forms,
morphing into one another
like the wind
were moving ghosts
across the town
and I was nothing but a bystander
wanting to watch the show
that the Gods were putting on-
telling an abstract tale in the sky
that only a child would understand.

Dying Adolescence

I spent my youth picking flowers and weeds
in a world undisturbed and still.
The sweet pleasures I miss
but like the myth of Sisyphus,
I'm stuck rolling a boulder up a hill.

A lament

Spike Jonze once wrote, "Sometimes I think I have felt everything I'm ever gonna feel. And from here on out, I'm not gonna feel anything new. Just lesser versions of what I've already felt."

It doesn't feel like Christmas anymore. The snowfall no longer looks like frost bit fairies, and my family's hallmark singing snowmen have sat in their boxes for years. The pinecones dressed in cinnamon and nutmeg reek of sentiment, flashing a radar in my mind. Calling out to me in third person. I am a stranger to my former- immune to magic, lost the ticket to wonderland, and can no longer hear the bell.

I think a child painted the world and man is always revising it.

I want to lift the veil that I've grown to see life through.

To taste an apple for the first time again. To look at the clouds and see Hercules, three blind mice, acrobats, and not a chamber of water. I want to be afraid of the dark. When I was certain monsters lied beneath me. Before the mind was touched by conceptions, and imagination bitten and corrupted by reality. When the map of this world was arcane, and every waking second a discovery.

I would live in a monastery, quarantined from the light, if one day I could step outside and be kissed by the sun like it was the first time.

I would starve myself just to value taste.

I'm afraid I'll die with this hunger. On my deathbed sitting with a waning heart longing to feel something new.

Paradise Regained

Where does the pavement end?
I'm tired of walking
carrying my own head.
Can I fall off the face of the world
and back into its hands
to be rocked back to sleep
never leaving dreamland.

Runaway

I've been given fields to roam,
streetlights designed
for the midnight kind
to find our way through the dark.
Pathways to heaven's gates surround me,

Yet I still feel the burning desire to flee.

Untitled

The void is becoming so large I don't know what to do with myself. I've tried gardening during each phase of the moon. And all I ask is to rest there soon.

Fools

My favorite night of my life
I skinny dipped in the Gulf of Mexico with a stranger.
We stood smiling at the moon
while being stirred within her waters.
I don't know what made him do it,
but for me,
this beam was looking back
at our naked selves-
dancing with her tides
and I thought that somehow
this was the witchcraft that would do it.
This potion
tango of three
Casting the miracle I've been searching for.
But the whole time we just stood stagnant beneath her.
    Our entire lives
    we are just stagnant beneath her.

Beyond my reach

Is it my fault
for passing all the wishing puffs?
Or moving to a city
where there are no shooting stars,
for blowing out every candle
and praying
for a pipe dream
time
and time again.
For only wanting
what God dangles
just beyond my reach

Eschaton

We're all suffering from a plague,
that only death can cure.
Can you feel the tilt of the axis,
and the ending of the world?

The Devil's Bird

Tell me something that I do not know, my little crow
Can you tell me where the sunlight seemed to go, my little crow

Are your midnight caws an echo of the Devil's desperate cries
And did you know that little songs my favorite lullaby

Why does the darkness call to us, like we're the shadows of the moon
Why do I feel my genetic strings are scratched and out of tune

I scavenge life like your own kind, never indulging in my own
But with your solace presence crow, I never feel alone

Thats why I always turn to you, seeking out for your advice
With all you've seen, could you just spare if life is worth the price

This feeling always lingers, like it's the nearing of the end
So tell me, tell me, tell me crow, is it time to be condemned

Seeking Self Help

Google suggest I start a garden.
Said life will bloom as long as I plant the seeds.
But the soil of mine has seemed to harden,
the only thing in the yard is tumbleweeds.

There's a fog in the way of the sun.
And poison ivy corrupted the court.
Howling winds steal my crops, leaving none.
Can"t be a gardener if I always fall short.

I don't own a shovel or hoe,
And it's been years living in this damn drought.
With no water nor tools I cant grow-
stuck in a hole and cant dig my way out.

But sometimes I witness seeds crack.
The better days when the flowers are born.
But every one step just leads me two back.
The petals fall and I'm pricked by the thorns.

I cant help but feel lost and behind.
Like I'm deaf to the world when it sings.
You cant harvest a cold winter mind.
Google tell me how does one become Spring?

The final act

The velvet curtains
swing to their sides
and spotlight
rests upon my back.
I pull the scroll
and read the words
Thus begins the final act.

I stand alone
I dance alone
the other cast
I had expelled.
A monodrama
a monastery-
they're all just
solo prison cells.

Hamlet's soliloquy-
To be or not to be,
But tell me
what's the purpose
to be
in solidarity?

If life is just a play
I've titled mine
the one man show

So when the curtains come down
and I take this bow
to a room
of empty seats,
I can tell you this is worse
than simply not to be.

Om

I took out my vocal chords
traded em' for brass strings.
No more weightless words,
wasted breaths,
in God's choir
I had learned to sing.
But the more that I would hum,
the more and more
I'd stand alone.
Oh I had lost my native tongue,
and I forgot the way back home.

Watching from the window

I haven't smelt the last burning days of autumn.
The bed of grass has frozen over
and the leaves have fallen without me.
A glass panel sits between us.
I've tried to write
to capture the slow dancing
of the snow,
the silence of this house
but it's taken two weeks
for my mind to have the strength
to battle
with an empty page.
My mother helps me wipe
my father hand feeds me my antidote-
I am a newborn again.
I cannot walk
cannot bathe
cannot dance
but watch the bare branches
do it without me.
The world is in motion
while I remain still.

Death

I didn't cry until I left the chapel. The last look I took of her face, pale and malnourished, frozen in place forever. I sat in the backseat, staring at an empty abandoned nest on the nearby oak, as my parents sat in silence. They didn't know how to console me, couldn't find nor drag out the words to describe what they both have felt before. Death is too short of a word. A jab. A period. The last punchline, despite it seeping and bleeding into everything.

Everything in life is like an open casket funeral. Looking through old photo albums. The final shedding of the last leaf on a branch. The nakedness of your childhood home, while watching a stranger paint over the growth markers on the doorframe. Old letters to myself, from myself, water slipping between the pages and washing away the ink. Tossing away the growing green tomatoes in the back of the fridge. Goodbyes and goodbyes and goodbyes all over again. I'm tired of always hand feeding the clock.

I sat in the backseat crying. My father turned the wheel and we drove away from the brick building and people walking out the doors, dressed in black, painted blue. For the first time in my life I got motion sickness. The rights and lefts down the dexter roads. And everything in life I'm passing by.

Infinite

There's a fog between me and the stars
and I'm starting to forget that they're there.

Clean Slate

Can I forget all I've forgotten?
My lost and found bin's thickening.
Can I forget all I remember,
each pair of eyes I've ever seen?
I'm a showcase of cold fingerprints,
I'm a living elegy.
Words of the dead lay on this skin
can I cleanse myself from me?

The past is like a shadow
I can't outrun
I'll never flee.
The present
a storage unit
of mothball stench
and history.

So tell me
where's the road, the route,
to the riverbank of lethe?
Take my wish of being swallowed
down the dark throat of the sea.
Every breath that's ever grazed my ear
quiet whispers
piercing screams.
Rushing waters of oblivion,
do me a favor
set me free.
I need a washing,
one last relief
I need to cleanse myself from me.

set me free

I keep screaming at a God
that I don't believe in.
Asking for a piece of heaven
but I'm just given
earth's address.
But if this
is the nearest
to the blissest
that it gets,
then take me to the chamber
where you store
the lost breaths.
I don't want to reincarnate
all I want's
eternal death.

On loneliness

"Hence in solitude, or that deserted state when we are surrounded by human beings and yet they sympathize not with us, we love the flowers, the grass, the waters, and the sky.

-Percy Shelley, On Love

What can a recluse do
but turn to the moon
or make a friend
of the mantis
and trees
But what does one do
when the half empty glass
can't even be filled
by the sea

Feeding the serpent

I came across a serpent in the garden
and told him my faith has been beat.
He said that he knows a way
but there must be a trade
so I told him off of me he can eat.

I keep feeding the serpent in the garden
so he comes back every morning to feast.
I've given all I've garnered
for its insatiable hunger
but the serpent will never be pleased.

I keep feeding the serpent in the garden
but it still devours everything it sees.
When I begin to chide
it bats it's wet eyes
and I see a little hurt girl like me.

Today I starved the serpent in the garden,
shut the gate and swallowed the key.
He's not my friend but the enemy
and his venom's not the remedy,
but if I don't kill him he'll kill me.

Ciphered tongue

I feel as if I'm existing on the cusp between life and death.
Always yielding when I open my mouth.

I wish I could speak, but only know how to in code-
of songs, or poems, or paintings, or prose.
I'm lost in translation
only my mind bears my name
the rest is all foreign, unfamiliar and of waste.

I wish I could speak, or make love, or breathe,
but I'm paying for experiences
with outdated currencies.

To write

The pen is nothing
but a double ended sword,
I live by drawing blood.

The imaginations
just a place of hiding
for those that have no one.

At the desk I sit
with myself at six
resurrection into ink.

I want to live
for eternity.
Immortalize me on a sheet.

a house that's never furnished

At the end of the rainbow road
there's a one house cul-de-sac.
Where the door is sealed and bolted
and lies a, *no ones welcome*, mat.

The walls are bleak and bare
with skeletons in every room.
I sit, my knees pressed to my chest
in this echo chamber tomb.

There's no relics of my life before
my scrapbooks full of empty pages.
I wish I salvaged souvenirs
and I wish I framed those faces.

I own a table made for one
and always eat at the head alone.
No light comes in the shaded windows,
it's a silent lifeless home.

I wish I had swallowed my pride
but all I did was just swallow the key.
My wind chimes are gone
so I sing the song-
the tune of woe it's me.

Winter

Naked limbs
stretching up towards the sky.
Pleading for something eternal.
Begging God
to not let the palmates drop.
Begging God
to allow them to hold on
to something forever.

Scarlett

We sat on the roof
with Ethel Cain and stolen weed.
Overlooking the city
at a height I've never seen.

We shared poems and song
and talked of all we can't possess.
Like the love of another
the moon forever at our left.

There's a silence in our speech
a hallow sound we try to cover.
We're barren and we're starved
feeding off the holes in each other.

Alienation

If I raise these hands high enough
can you take me?
All I ask is for relief-
an aid
for this insufficient reach.
To be meshed
and compressed
to be again
just one piece.

Four arms,
four legs,
til Zeus intervened.
A mosaic shattered
I'm left searching on my knees.
One umbilical chord
now an infinite of strings.
    So here I am
    reaching for everything.

Longing

Sometimes
it seems in another life
I was the last leaf on the branch
stretching and reaching
for your unknowing hand
on a more beautiful tree.

Adieu

I'd try to wish you well
but there's no wishing well
deep enough
to hold all I would say to you.

Who clipped her wings

An angel guided me
through the streets of Lesvos Greece.
Expanding my world
in the span of three weeks.
She knew every constellation
Orion and Perseus,
now all I see is her cursive name
when I look up at the sky.

One Saturday night
after the sun went to sleep,
we shuffled Bon Iver
from Skinny Love to Holocene.
But when he sang the first verse
she threw her head on her knees
and let out the whole cosmos
through her golden brown eyes.

Why do the greatest souls
carry the world on their shoulders?
Why are the toughest battles
toppled on the sweetest soldiers?
Why is there nothing I can do
but drop my arms and simply hold her?
Why must you shed the whole sea
But always wipe my own eyes dry?

Her cheeks were flushed out red
and veins ready to explode.
I watched her clench her throat
and crystal tears begin to flow.
Said that the moon was too full,
and now it's just too large to hold.
I cannot watch you bear the world
Angel, pick up your wings and fly.

Letter to Mom

What if this sickness takes you
before you cure your own?
The one that was passed down to me.
What if this sickness takes you
Before you kiss all my wounds
before you ever mouth the words
I'm sorry

What if this sickness takes you
before I set free the grudge
I've been hauling for seventeen years?
When I'm holding your hand
I'll dig my nail in your palms
or scream
in your feeble ears.

What if this sickness takes you
before you get the chance to change,
before you heal yourself
from the ancestral pain
and I walk my whole life
with my feet balled and chained
and I'll forever feel a burn
when I hear your first name.

What if this sickness takes you
before I learn how to grieve
and all the good we once shared
I turn into spite.
I am a selfish child
making your cancer about me
but I'm afraid to be left stranded
dying in wait for the light.

Contortion

You were my favorite figment
of the imagination.
A character I wrote
in fantasy fiction.
I dreamt
your green eyes pink
and crystalline,
and your own dreams different
than you wanted them to be.

You were a
rubber band
I'd stretch and bend
to fit around my wrist.
But I'm a hypocrite
and tossed you
when the rubber split
and I am so
so sorry.

A testament to motherhood

I asked my mother
if she'd do it all again.
If she'd sacrifice herself
for the breath of her kids,
if she'd walk a different path
if the past she could re-live.
She said there's not a better gift
that any God could give.

When you fed all my dreams
the trade was starving yours.
You bled your whole life
just for me to be born.
And was a piece of you lost
to the umbilical chord?
I often think that my birth
was when the old you was mourned.

You cut and pierced your fingers
when you threaded this home.
And the cartilage I stand with
I took from your backbone.
Motherhood is like a lump sum
Where you give all that you own-
even down to your last name
even down to your throne.

I watch you drop all your wants
to place the food on our plates.
I watch your eyes grow bags
and the emerald in them fade.
And how your shoulders hang low
from carrying the world's weight.
Do you want more than "great mom"
on the head of your grave?

I know that if a God is real
she'd take the form of a mother.
Women nailed into the cross
for the good of another.
Having to bury themselves
to hold up the grounds above her.
Mom you deserve the world
but the world watches you suffer.

Family heirloom

We fight
at two heads
of the same table
as the water trembles
in its glass.

You use to say
that you gave me my voice,
but when I took it back
it began to sound like yours.
I am a child of echolalia-
mirroring your tongue
I hear
through the willow glass walls.

I guess fury is our family heirloom.
I hate how I pocket
anger in my cheeks
and blood
between my teeth
and how my jaw stays clenched
every night when I sleep,
and how I'm living
a historic reoccurrence
of the man across the table.

He is not my savior

In a cabin in Wisconsin, I was told about God. Women who held their bibles to their chests like it were armor, gathered to spread his word in the woods. After every meal we'd turn on hymns and they would belt to the sky. Their fingers were intertwined, heads rested on another's shoulder. I stood watching, an outlier to their circle. I'd rub my fingers on my iris- hoping to drag out a tear, but all I ever felt was envy in their faith.

One night, my cabin leader took me aside and told me that I'm walking with the antichrists. That I keep throwing my ticket to the gates away, but I'm always offered readmission with the prayer of salvation. If I tell him I believe the words of Moses, and all the other people that sounded like distant concepts to me, he'd place my name-tag at the dining table. So I did. I would beg on my knees time and time again- a stack of unopened letters on his desk. But I never felt a thing, and I knew I would never be granted a seat.

I ASK TO REMAIN UNTITLED

Two autumns ago, I was sitting along this river in my backyard.
The grass tucked beneath a bed of decaying leaves,
The fall wind tossing them around.
    I've seen it all before.
Curious to know if not seeing at all,
would guide me into seeing in a new light,
I shut my eyes.
And as the fallen leaves became tap-dancers beginning their show,
their delicate feet making music on the ground,
I couldn't help but wonder why we call them leaves anyway,
and not a song.

Down on the riverbed, I watched all sorts of life gathering around.
Fleeing the closer I got, vanishing when my presence interfered with theirs.
Was this act an attempt at swimming against the current of man?
Swimming away from the hands that try to grab you with these tongs
and slap you on some encyclopedia page.
A page that tells *you* what *you* are.
    A fish:
        a limbless <u>cold-blooded</u> <u>vertebrate</u> animal with <u>gills</u> and fins and
        living wholly in water.
A title and fate set in stone.
Now incapable of being anything less.
Now incapable of being anything more.

I wish my mom called me by her own name.
"I love you Diane"
"Nothing's out to get you Diane"
Could hearing her own be used with some grace of the tongue
make her smile in the mirror?
Would she understand how much she glows
if she saw herself in every light she stood before?
If every wildflower,
and lightning bug,
and shooting star
were called, *Diane*,
would she then know
that she does not have to live bound to something?

Should I have called her more than just mom?

So call me a dragonfly tomorrow, and a bastard today,
call me an egg,
call me the yolk,
call me a burden, and a blessing,
and anything and everything,
for I do not want to be stuck in a body
stuck with one name.

Don't want my voice to stand out

but to blend with the wind
one wouldn't tell
if it's their mother's
or the sparrow's song
or the floorboards
creaking
speaking
below.

Lost in the city of angels

I kissed the lips of the envelope
that I sent from L.A,
and I pocketed every peony
that passed upon my way.

But if the petals are all withered
by the time I make it home,
nurse them with my sorrows
and every piece of me you own.

I've confided in every chaplain
on how to free me from your clutch,
but I am cursed by inability
to live without your touch.

A requiem of us

I had a dream that I was with you
light was pouring from your head.
And when I woke, I saw your shadow
near the footrest of my bed.

Do you remember sneaking out at night
when we'd dance on frozen lakes?
Or rest our heads on beds of grass
And lie, stargazing in the rain.

We were outliers on the graph
who walked the opposite of reason.
We broke the clock, and dared our odds
but now I'm programmed with the seasons.

When I moved to New York,
I sent you letters in the post.
Said that, *death can't even part us*
For I'll be haunted by your ghost.

In the bass of my old radio
I feel the beating of your heart.
In the craters of the moon
I see your dimples, your beauty marks.

Your hair hangs from the willows
my sheets feel like your skin
your voice I hear in strangers
your fragrance in the wind.

You made a map of my subconscious
there's not a place that I can hide in.
Where I go, your footsteps follow
despite the distance and the silence.

So if I never hear your laugh
that sacred soothing hymn,
I know I'll see you in my dreams
and when it all begins again.

My own memorabilia

I want to put the past in a mason jar. Or put it in words and place it under my pillow. to live it all again.

You lead me to a place that soon became "our" island. It was a hideout painted by Monet / We'd climb the pyramid of straw and hay as mom took a picture of us- a postcard and testament to our youth / I spent a week biking along the Florida coast in April. Before sunrise, after sunset, we'd fill the baskets with fruit and have a picnic on the beach / I'm a sucker for spring, and all things gifted second chances. Another go around.

I want to live it all again

You got me in the habit of flipping one cigarette for good luck / We rushed out the exit door on the subway and stood on the small bridge between the cars. The whole city unfolded before our eyes / The bar was closing, but we didn't wanna leave. We lied down and stamped ourselves on the disco floor / Your eyes were vermillion beneath the blood moon / It was after midnight and the Parthenon was staring at us in the face on the rooftop bar. The present threaded by the past / I flip the cigarette and think of you.

I want to live it all again

We caught up at a sushi bar in midtown. Looking back on the days when you being here was more than a weekend vacation. When we would sleep in the same twin size bed, and walk the naked streets for tea at dawn.

I want to live it all again

On the ferry ride to Lesvos, we stayed up all night and watched the sun play hide and seek behind the Greek mountains. We sat silently on our folding chairs, listening to the Past Lives soundtrack, heading to a place unknown to us / Wordsworth says our life is but a sleep and a forgetting, but all I want is to remember / The sunset washes the day / The incense turns to dust.

I want to live it all again

Pantheism

Take me to the wailing wall.
Let us not bow our heads
but scream in sync-
crack and crumble
the stack of stone,
and to see that God lies
in the front of our throats.

Word of God

Book of Foukyon. 7:20

In Lesvos, the student housing I stayed at was overlooked by an old, tender man. We soon formed a bond, and he carved time out of his nights to teach me the traditional Greek dances. We'd line up, wrap our arms around each others shoulders, and step to the songs. The pavilion was our stage and we were performing for the stars. I barely knew how to speak Greek, I felt like your typical midwestern fool, but we would communicate through the rhythm and movement of our bodies. Twisting, breaking through the language barrier with our feet; It became our evening routine.

Today we're separated by the sea, and I often turn on the melodies to dance alone in my home. But I still feel his presence. His hand rested on my shoulder.

Book of Audrey. 12:30

My little sister always loved the company of another. Her childhood friends have slept in her bed as many times as she had. When the floors of our house were rattling, the beams breaking, falling apart, she'd stay with one of her companions. Seeking light in dark times and losing herself and her worries in the face of another. I often tell her that she's like a seamstress, sewing back the umbilical cord, preferring to be conjoined than in isolation. Through everything she does, I can see that love is what leads her. And each day I am granted the gift to be beside her, I understand the concept of it more.

Book of the orchestra. 2:18

    Two months into New York, I went to the Lincoln Center with my art class. I took mushrooms shortly before, and every second leading to being seated I wanted to pull trig. I get motion sickness in crowds when I'm clear headed, so being engulfed in a cacophony of voices, under the vice of this little fungus was more than enough to leave my shoulders perched beside my ears. Until I made my way to my seat, and a hush fell over the room. The performers came out, sat in their positions, as the conductor emerged from behind the podium.

    After the final standing ovation, I felt my eyes well up, and my smile lines catch its fall. I had witnessed the absolute- 50 instruments, 100 different hands, one mesmeric voice.

Book of the Persian rug. 11:11

    There's a universe within my carpet. Microscopic dust speckles surfing on the creases and folds.

Book of Tim. 3:16

    Everywhere he went, he traveled barefoot. Foot soles on soil, soil on the soles. During the full moon when the beam made a path along the water's surface, he stood in it and made an open spot for me. We rested in her light, cleansed by the mother of all mothers. Just two children beneath her. He always wore a harmonica around his neck, and took it out at times when most would pick up their phones. The group we were with called him the spirit of our batch, and each of us pocketed some of his cosmic dust to rub and spread on our skin in times when we needed it.

Book of Benjamin Moore. 4:12

    Mr. Moore is a guideman. He was a professor who taught me more in four months than all of my own efforts in my 18 years. During our habitual walks in central park, our young adult field trips, you could see how every sound and color that washed over him, he so deeply wished to bathe in.

One afternoon, we stopped amongst a playground and all of our thoughts seemed to be lifted from us. We watched the children create a whirlwind of light around the tire swings, and their laughs spread a childlike innocence to the rest of the park. He broke our silence with the words I hope to never forget. That these children "were more like plants than they are of man". That they do not quench to know, or crave to solve some mystery, but simply love to lie in it. Ever since then, I try and tell myself to act like a child. To live freely and foolishly- to be a lily, four leaf clover, that single hair of grass, blowing in the wind.

Book of Me. 12:24

Around 12 I stopped praying at the dining table. I told my mom it seemed forced, like I'm knocking on the door of a vacant house. I wondered why we cast our heads down, instead of looking at each other. Why we're told we only know God if we pick up the book. Once I began to pick up my head, I started seeing her everywhere. In the forms and conversations with another, I feel I learned more than some verse could ever offer. For in your iris I see the moon. And in your voice I hear the sound of God.

www.ingramcontent.com/pod-product-compliance
Lightning Source LLC
Chambersburg PA
CBHW032217040426
42449CB00005B/646